Zack Polanski Biography

A British Politician's Journey in the Green Party, Climate Change Leadership, and the Fight for Social and Environmental Justice

Marina Wynford

Zack Polanski Biography

Copyright © 2025 Marina Wynford

Table of Contents

Table of Contents 1
Introduction 3
Chapter One 6
   The Making of Zack Polanski 6
Chapter Two 16
   From Salford Streets to Center Stage 16
Chapter Three 26
   A Life in Performance: Acting, Art, and Self-Discovery 26
Chapter Four 36
   Reinvention and Resilience 36
Chapter Five 47
   The Leap Into Politics 47
Chapter Six 57
   Finding a Home in the Green Party 57
Chapter Seven 68
   A Voice for London 68
Chapter Eight 79
   The Rise of an Eco-Populist 79
Chapter Nine 90
   Leadership, Vision, and the Fight for Justice 90
Chapter Ten 100
   Hope as a Political Force 100
Conclusion 111

Introduction

Every generation produces a handful of voices that rise above the noise—voices that don't just talk about change but embody it. Zack Polanski is one of those rare voices. From the gritty streets of Salford to the very heart of London's political stage, his journey has been nothing short of extraordinary. He didn't come from privilege, nor did he follow the polished path of career politicians. Instead, Zack carved his own road—through art, activism, and sheer determination—until he stood at the helm of one of the fastest-growing political movements in Britain: the Green Party.

This isn't just the story of a politician. It's the story of a man who dares to reimagine what leadership looks like in the 21st century. Zack Polanski speaks not from ivory towers but from the lived realities of ordinary people—the struggles of paying rent, the urgency of climate change, the heartbreak of inequality. He embodies a brand of politics rooted in authenticity, compassion, and an unshakable belief that no one should ever be left behind.

Why should you keep reading? Because Zack's story is also about you. It's about what's possible when courage outweighs fear, when purpose outshines doubt, and when one person decides to step into the arena and fight for a better tomorrow. His life is a testament to resilience, to the power of reinvention, and to the radical idea that politics can still serve people rather than power.

So, turn the page. Lean in. Let this book challenge you, inspire you, maybe even unsettle you—but most of all, let it remind you that one determined individual can ignite a movement. Zack Polanski's journey is proof that hope, when paired with action, can change the world.

Chapter One

The Making of Zack Polanski

The story of Zack Polanski begins not in a grand political chamber or under the bright lights of television cameras, but in the streets of Salford, a city known for its grit, resilience, and working-class character. Growing up in such a place, one learns quickly about the realities of life—struggles, perseverance, and the sheer determination required to carve out something better. For Zack, the formative years were never about privilege or inherited opportunity. They were about finding a voice in the midst of noise, shaping an identity in a world that demanded toughness, and recognizing early on that if he wanted to change his circumstances, he would have to summon a strength from within that few could see but he always carried.

Childhood was marked by curiosity. Zack was never content simply to accept things at face value. He asked questions others might hesitate to pose. Why were some families comfortable while others scraped by? Why did certain people have the freedom to dream while others were confined by circumstance? Those questions were more than the idle wanderings of a child's mind; they were the sparks of a restless spirit, the kind that would later demand accountability from political leaders and refuse to accept the status quo. In Salford, where the distance between hardship and hope could be measured in footsteps, young Zack was already mapping out a different kind of journey.

He found early refuge in imagination. Storytelling and performance became more than hobbies; they became ways of surviving, of making sense of a complicated world. Teachers noticed his ability to step into roles with confidence, his capacity to transform a room not by force but by presence. It was clear that while some children turned inward, Zack turned outward. He wanted to engage, to connect, to understand people on a deeper level. That yearning for connection would later define not just his artistic pursuits but also his political life.

As adolescence arrived, Zack was drawn into the performing arts with a seriousness that surprised even those closest to him. Acting was not just about applause or attention. It was about empathy. Every role required him to step into another's shoes, to live through another's eyes, to experience the world from a perspective outside his own. That discipline—learning to feel the struggles and joys of others—was a training ground for the empathy he would one day bring into politics. Unlike the detached style of many career politicians, Zack's roots were firmly planted in this ability to see people, really see them, and then reflect that understanding back in a way that mattered.

But it wasn't just performance that shaped his early identity. Growing up in a diverse, often challenging environment taught him resilience. In neighborhoods where opportunity was scarce, and where ambition often collided with the heavy weight of reality, Zack had to learn how to reinvent himself constantly. Reinvention would become a defining theme of his life. Each chapter, whether in art, psychotherapy, or politics, carried with it a willingness to step into the unknown, to embrace change not as a threat but as a path forward.

His time as a young man also carried moments of uncertainty. Acting can be a brutal profession, one that demands both vulnerability and steel. Rejection, criticism, and the constant need to prove oneself were daily realities. Yet Zack found in those challenges a deeper strength. Rather than letting rejection silence him, he let it sharpen him. He learned how to stand tall in the face of doubt, how to move forward even when doors closed. That inner resolve became an armor—not a barrier, but a shield that allowed him to keep pursuing the roles that mattered, both on stage and in life.

Behind the curtain of performance, however, another side of Zack was emerging. While acting gave him a voice, it was his fascination with people's inner lives that began to take hold. He saw how emotions, struggles, and unspoken battles shaped every individual he encountered. This curiosity wasn't idle; it led him toward a path of studying the mind and eventually working as a psychotherapist. That shift revealed yet another layer of his making. Where once he had stood on stage to portray others, now he sat with people to help them face their own truths.

That work was not glamorous, but it was transformative. Listening to people's pain, guiding them through moments of crisis, and holding space for their growth gave Zack a profound sense of purpose. It taught him patience, discipline, and the rare ability to remain present. More importantly, it reinforced a belief that every voice mattered, that every person carried a story worth hearing. Later, when he entered politics, this training as a listener distinguished him from the many who entered with speeches but not with ears.

Zack's Jewish heritage also played a role in shaping his perspective. Growing up with an awareness of cultural history, of resilience forged through generations, gave him a connection to identity and justice that he never ignored. The traditions of community, the lessons of endurance, and the emphasis on responsibility to others were woven into the fabric of his upbringing. These values were not abstract; they were lived. They gave him a compass, one that would later guide him through the complexities of political life without losing sight of his moral bearings.

By the time Zack began to step into the public arena, he had already lived several lives. Actor, therapist, activist—each identity shaped the one that followed, layering experience upon experience until he became something more than the sum of his parts. He carried with him the artistry of performance, the empathy of healing, and the fire of a restless spirit unwilling to stand by while the world faltered.

The making of Zack Polanski is not the story of a straight line. It is the story of twists, turns, setbacks, and breakthroughs. It is about the boy from Salford who refused to stay silent, the young man who learned to navigate rejection without losing his voice, the therapist who held others through their pain, and the leader who emerged with a vision that change was not only necessary but possible. In each of these stages, one thing remained constant: a refusal to settle for less than the truth, a commitment to living fully, and a determination to shape the world rather than simply endure it.

Chapter Two

From Salford Streets to Center Stage

Salford was not the kind of place where dreams were handed out. It was a city of brick terraces and working-class determination, where people carried resilience like a second skin. For a boy like Zack Polanski, the streets offered lessons every bit as valuable as the ones found inside a classroom. They were crowded, noisy, sometimes unforgiving, but they also held sparks of possibility for anyone daring enough to look. Zack was one of those kids who noticed things others overlooked—the laughter behind hardship, the beauty in small gestures, and the courage of people who fought every day to make ends meet.

Growing up, his world was defined by contrasts. On one hand, there was the weight of economic struggle that surrounded so many families, a reminder that survival often came before ambition. On the other, there was a pulse of creativity and culture, the sense that stories could lift people above the grind of daily life. For Zack, those contrasts shaped a unique outlook. He didn't just see the limits; he also saw the potential to break through them.

Even as a child, he was drawn to performance. He could imitate voices, play characters, and command attention in a way that seemed natural. What others saw as a pastime, Zack treated as a kind of calling.

He discovered early on that standing in front of people, telling a story, or slipping into a role wasn't simply about entertaining—it was about connection. It was about making people feel something, about giving them a glimpse of another world. In Salford, where many carried heavy burdens, that ability mattered. It gave him a way to shine light into places that often felt dark.

The local community offered both challenges and opportunities. Resources were limited, but there were teachers and mentors who spotted his spark and encouraged him to lean into it. He wasn't the loudest or the most obvious star, but he carried a depth that caught attention. He worked hard, rehearsed relentlessly, and treated every small stage like it was the most important platform in the world. That seriousness separated him from peers who thought of acting as just another after-school activity. For Zack, it was never a hobby—it was preparation.

Adolescence brought new layers of complexity. While many of his friends were drawn into the routine of ordinary jobs or the pull of street life, Zack's gaze was elsewhere. He wanted to explore beyond the narrow expectations that often boxed in kids from his background. He didn't just want stability; he wanted expression, impact, the kind of life that left a mark. That ambition, however, came with sacrifices. It meant standing apart, pursuing a path few around him understood, and taking risks that might lead to failure. But Zack had already decided that failure was not the enemy. Complacency was.

The leap from Salford to the wider world of performance wasn't simple. Auditions brought rejection more often than applause. Casting directors measured him not just by talent but by type, and the industry had a way of closing doors before they fully opened. Still, he kept pushing. Each rejection was a bruise, but never a defeat. He learned to walk out of auditions with his head high, ready for the next opportunity. That kind of resilience—honed on stage and sharpened by experience—would later serve him well in the brutal world of politics.

Zack's acting career took him to unexpected places. He found himself in roles that demanded intensity, vulnerability, and absolute commitment. Every character required research, discipline, and a willingness to dig into emotions most people spend their lives avoiding. Audiences responded not just to his performances but to the authenticity behind them. He wasn't trying to impress; he was trying to reveal something real. That instinct—honesty over show—was rare in an industry often built on appearances.

Yet behind the curtain, the lessons ran deeper. Performance taught him discipline: the endless rehearsals, the precision of timing, the awareness that every detail mattered. It also taught him adaptability. A stage actor learns quickly that no two audiences are alike. Energy shifts, reactions differ, and success depends on the ability to read a room and adjust in real time. Those skills—reading people, sensing undercurrents, shifting strategy without losing authenticity—would later define his style in debates, interviews, and political campaigns.

But acting was never just about craft. For Zack, it was also about freedom. The stage became a space where he could transcend the limits of his background, where he could reimagine himself in infinite ways. It was a declaration that identity wasn't fixed, that people could transform, grow, and step into new versions of themselves whenever they chose. This philosophy—of reinvention as a form of survival and power—would echo through his later career shifts, from acting to therapy to politics.

Salford never left him, though. No matter how far he traveled or how bright the lights became, the city was etched into his DNA. Its toughness, its humor, its raw honesty stayed with him. He carried the memory of neighbors who worked long hours, of families who counted every penny, of friends who dreamed big but settled small because opportunity never knocked. Those memories didn't weigh him down; they fueled him. They were reminders of why his voice mattered, why he couldn't simply pursue personal success without considering the bigger picture.

The journey from Salford streets to the stage was more than a career move. It was a declaration of possibility. It said that a kid from a working-class city could stand in front of audiences and command their attention, that his story was worth telling, that his presence mattered. In many ways, stepping onto the stage was Zack's first political act, even if he didn't realize it at the time. It was the moment he learned that visibility is power, that storytelling can shift minds, and that one voice, used well, can change the entire atmosphere of a room.

Those early years built the foundation for everything that followed. They taught him grit, empathy, resilience, and the courage to embrace reinvention. They revealed the power of presence and the responsibility of voice. They shaped a boy from Salford into a man ready to stand not just on stage but eventually in the political spotlight, carrying with him the lessons of where he came from and the promise of where he was determined to go.

Chapter Three

A Life in Performance: Acting, Art, and Self-Discovery

The curtain rises, the lights sharpen, and a hush settles over the room. For Zack Polanski, moments like these were not just performances—they were revelations. Every time he stepped onto a stage, he carried more than lines to recite. He carried questions about who he was, who he could become, and how art could unlock truths hidden beneath the surface of daily life. Acting was never simply a career choice. It was a vehicle for transformation, both for the audience and for himself.

The early years in performance were marked by a relentless hunger to learn. Zack understood quickly that acting was not about pretending; it was about uncovering. A character wasn't a mask to hide behind but a doorway into a new layer of human experience. He studied people closely—how they spoke, how they moved, the subtle ways they revealed pain or joy without saying a word. He turned those observations into tools, weaving them into roles that demanded honesty. For Zack, truth was the heartbeat of performance. Anything less felt hollow.

The theater, with its immediacy and intimacy, became his training ground. On stage, there were no edits, no retakes, no protective screens. The connection with the audience was raw and alive, shifting with every breath. Zack thrived in that environment. He relished the unpredictability, the challenge of sustaining energy across long performances, the discipline required to remain present no matter what distractions arose. It was in those moments of vulnerability—standing exposed under the lights—that he discovered strength he never knew he possessed.

Each role offered a new form of self-discovery. Playing a character meant diving into unfamiliar worlds, wrestling with emotions that weren't his own, and allowing those emotions to alter him in return. He didn't just portray lives; he absorbed them. A role could linger for weeks, sometimes months, reshaping how he viewed himself and others. Through art, Zack learned that identity is fluid, that people contain multitudes, and that empathy is not optional but essential. These insights would later infuse his politics with a rare authenticity, but at the time, they were lessons in the art of being human.

Yet performance wasn't confined to the stage. Zack found meaning in the broader world of art—in storytelling, in music, in creative expression of all kinds. Art gave him language when words fell short. It gave him permission to feel deeply in a society that often demanded restraint. Most of all, it gave him a mirror. Every performance reflected something back to him: a fear he hadn't faced, a strength he hadn't recognized, a truth he hadn't yet accepted. The stage was not an escape from reality; it was a way of engaging with it more fully.

Of course, the life of an actor was not without struggle. Auditions were nerve-wracking battlegrounds, where talent was weighed against appearance, timing, and luck. Rejection came often and without explanation. It was a profession where "no" was heard far more than "yes." But Zack refused to let those setbacks diminish him. Each rejection became fuel, sharpening his resolve. He approached every opportunity with the same intensity, whether the role was grand or modest, because he understood that growth came not from applause but from practice.

The discipline of performance demanded sacrifice. Long hours of rehearsal, endless memorization, and the physical toll of embodying characters tested his endurance. Yet Zack embraced the grind. He knew that excellence wasn't born from talent alone; it was forged in repetition, sweat, and the willingness to push beyond comfort. This mindset, shaped by the rigors of acting, became a cornerstone of his character. When later confronted with the complexities of public service, he carried the same discipline into the political arena, refusing to settle for half-measures.

What made Zack stand out as a performer was not flamboyance but sincerity. Audiences sensed it.

They could feel the difference between an actor delivering lines and an actor living them. Zack belonged to the latter. He treated each role as an act of service, a chance to make people think, laugh, cry, or reconsider their own lives. That dedication to meaning over spectacle drew respect from colleagues and audiences alike. He wasn't chasing fame; he was chasing depth.

But art was not only about craft and discipline. It was also about liberation. On stage, Zack found the freedom to test boundaries, to inhabit identities far from his own, to question the norms that society imposed. Each performance was an act of exploration, peeling back the layers of convention and expectation. For someone who grew up in a city where options often felt limited, art was expansive. It proved that identity was not fixed by birthplace or circumstance but could be constantly rewritten through courage and imagination.

At the same time, performance sharpened his understanding of vulnerability. To act well required exposure, the willingness to be seen in raw, unfiltered ways. Audiences connected not to perfection but to openness. That realization seeped into his personal life, teaching him that strength is not the absence of weakness but the courage to reveal it. In politics, that belief would later separate him from leaders who built walls of rhetoric and ego. Zack's instinct was always to tear down walls, not to build them.

Art also introduced him to the community. The theater was a place where collaboration reigned. No performance succeeded through one person alone; it depended on trust, timing, and mutual support. Zack thrived in that environment, valuing the collective effort as much as his individual role. He carried that lesson forward, believing that progress—whether artistic or political—was born not from solitary genius but from people working together with a shared purpose.

Self-discovery through performance was not a single epiphany but a continuous unfolding. Each script, each rehearsal, each audience offered another piece of the puzzle. Zack came to see performance as a mirror reflecting back the endless complexity of human life. The struggles, the triumphs, the contradictions—all of it played out on stage, and all of it left an imprint on him.

The stage gave him more than applause. It gave him perspective. It revealed the power of storytelling to shift minds and open hearts. It showed him that a single voice, delivered with honesty, could ripple through a crowd and linger long after the final bow. And it taught him, perhaps most importantly, that identity is not static. A person can evolve, reinvent, and discover new dimensions of themselves through the courage to step into the unknown.

Chapter Four

Reinvention and Resilience

Life rarely moves in straight lines. For Zack Polanski, the path forward was never about clinging to one identity or one definition of success. His story is a testament to the power of change, the willingness to take risks, and the determination to rise each time the world tested his resolve. Reinvention was not a side note in his life—it was the theme. And resilience was the glue that held it all together.

After years in performance, Zack could have stayed on stage indefinitely. He had talent, he had discipline, and he had the passion to keep pursuing roles. But there was a restless energy in him, a voice that kept whispering that there was more. Acting was rewarding, but it wasn't enough. The applause ended when the curtain fell, and Zack was left with bigger questions: What impact was he truly making? Was he simply entertaining, or was he changing lives? That search for deeper purpose pushed him toward reinvention.

The transition was not smooth. Reinvention never is. Walking away from something familiar meant starting over, often with little certainty about where the next chapter would lead. For Zack, that meant stepping into psychotherapy, a world that demanded a completely different kind of discipline. On stage, he had learned to inhabit characters and reveal truths through performance. In therapy, he learned to step back, to listen, and to help others uncover their own truths. The spotlight shifted, and Zack chose not to stand in it but to hold it steady for others.

Becoming a psychotherapist required more than curiosity—it required commitment. Training was rigorous, filled with endless study, practical work, and emotional intensity. Zack leaned into it fully, knowing that the skill of truly listening to another human being was as important as any craft he had honed before. He found himself sitting with people at their most vulnerable, navigating pain, confusion, and trauma. These were not scripted lines or staged emotions; they were raw, real, and unfiltered. His role was not to fix but to guide, not to perform but to witness.

In those sessions, Zack discovered resilience of another kind. It was no longer about enduring rejection from casting directors or pushing through the exhaustion of rehearsals. It was about holding space for people when they were breaking apart, staying steady when their worlds were crumbling. The work demanded empathy, patience, and a refusal to shy away from discomfort. It also taught him that resilience is not only personal—it can be shared, nurtured, and built together.

Yet reinvention did not stop there. The more Zack listened to individual struggles, the more he began to see patterns. People were not suffering in isolation; they were suffering because of broader systems that failed them. Housing insecurity, poverty, discrimination, and inequality weren't abstract issues—they were daily realities for the people who sat across from him. Therapy was powerful, but it could only reach one person at a time. Zack began to feel an undeniable pull toward something larger: the world of politics, where change could be scaled, where policies could shape lives before they broke apart.

Making the leap into politics was another reinvention, one that demanded resilience on an entirely new scale. Unlike the stage or the therapy room, politics was a battlefield where criticism came loud and public, where motives were questioned, and where wins were never guaranteed. Zack entered that world not with naivety but with conviction. He understood that his strength lay not in pretending to have all the answers but in his ability to connect, to listen, and to channel people's concerns into action.

The resilience he had cultivated through earlier chapters of his life became his armor. The rejection from acting taught him how to handle political setbacks without losing confidence. The emotional intensity of therapy prepared him to deal with the complexities of people's struggles without flinching. The grit from Salford gave him the toughness to withstand criticism without losing his humanity.

Each reinvention wasn't a departure from the past; it was a layering of experiences, each one adding weight and depth to the man he was becoming.

But resilience, for Zack, was never about hardening or shutting down. It was about flexibility. It was about absorbing blows without breaking, adapting to circumstances without losing core values, and constantly finding new ways to grow. Where some people saw failure, he saw an opportunity to pivot. Where others clung to one identity, Zack embraced the possibility of many. Reinvention was his way of resisting stagnation, and resilience was the tool that kept him moving forward.

The challenges were constant. Entering politics meant facing a world dominated by established parties, entrenched interests, and leaders who often saw newcomers as nuisances rather than equals. Zack had to prove himself, not through connections or privilege, but through authenticity. His background didn't look like the polished résumés of career politicians. He wasn't groomed for leadership. He built himself piece by piece, reinvention by reinvention, until his story itself became a source of credibility. People could see he wasn't pretending; he was living proof that change was possible.

That authenticity resonated. While some dismissed him as inexperienced, others saw in him the kind of leader politics desperately needed: someone unafraid to step outside the script, someone willing to adapt, someone whose resilience had been tested in real ways. Each reinvention—actor, therapist, activist, politician—added to his arsenal. He wasn't confined to one world; he could move between them, draw lessons from each, and weave them into a vision bigger than himself.

Resilience also meant enduring criticism without losing direction. Politics invites cynicism, and Zack faced plenty of it. There were those who doubted his motives, those who dismissed his background, and those who underestimated his staying power. But he never defined himself by what others thought. He returned again and again to the lessons of his past: the stage that taught him presence, the therapy room that taught him listening, the streets of Salford that taught him toughness. These weren't just experiences—they were anchors.

In each chapter of his life, Zack had been forced to ask hard questions: Who am I when the role ends? Who am I when the audience leaves? Who am I when someone sits across from me in pain? Who am I when the world tells me I don't belong in politics? Each reinvention offered an answer, and each answer made him stronger.

The making of Zack Polanski is inseparable from the pattern of transformation. His story is not about clinging to a single identity but about embracing the courage to change. It is about learning to bend without breaking, to evolve without losing authenticity, and to rise after every setback with renewed determination. Reinvention gave him new paths; resilience made sure he could walk them.

Chapter Five

The Leap Into Politics

There comes a moment in every life when the path ahead splits, when comfort and certainty sit on one side, and risk and possibility lie on the other. For Zack Polanski, that moment came with an undeniable pull toward politics. His earlier chapters—performance, therapy, activism—had already prepared him to see the world differently. He had felt the struggles of ordinary people, seen their frustrations up close, and understood that individual effort alone was not enough. If real change was going to happen, it had to come from a place where systems were built, rules were shaped, and voices could be amplified. That place was politics.

Stepping into politics was not a casual decision. It was bold, uncertain, and fraught with challenges. Zack knew full well what the political arena looked like: combative, dominated by insiders, often cynical and resistant to newcomers. But he also knew that if people like him didn't step forward, the same old patterns would continue. He didn't wait for an invitation. He chose to leap.

His entry into politics didn't begin in a grand hall or on a national stage—it started at the grassroots level. Campaigns on clean air, housing rights, and climate justice became his training ground. He stood on street corners, knocked on doors, and listened to Londoners who felt abandoned by traditional parties. Those conversations were raw and unfiltered. Parents worried about asthma rates in children living near polluted roads. Tenants spoke of landlords raising rents while neglecting basic repairs. Young people questioned whether they would ever own a home or even afford stable rent. These weren't abstract policy debates; they were lived realities. Zack absorbed them, and they fueled his conviction that politics had to be more than speeches and slogans. It had to be action.

When Zack aligned himself with the Green Party, it wasn't because it was the easy route. The Greens were not the dominant force in British politics.

They didn't have the resources of larger parties or the weight of longstanding power structures behind them. What they did have was authenticity, a commitment to social and environmental justice, and a willingness to speak truth where others dodged. For Zack, that mattered more than comfort. Joining the Green Party was a declaration that politics should serve people and the planet, not just the privileged few.

His leap into electoral politics tested every ounce of resilience he had built. Campaigning was exhausting. Days stretched into nights filled with strategy meetings, canvassing, and public debates. He had to prove himself to skeptical voters, many of whom had never heard of him before. He relied not on polished sound bites but on sincerity. He spoke plainly, avoided jargon, and leaned into his strength: listening. When people felt heard, they began to believe he could represent them.

Zack's leap wasn't just about personal ambition—it was about reimagining politics itself. He challenged the idea that leadership had to come from elites groomed for power. He showed that someone with a background in acting and therapy, someone who had walked the streets of Salford and worked with ordinary Londoners, could stand for office and do it with integrity. That message resonated with those who felt politics had left them behind.

The leap also demanded courage in facing critics. There were those who dismissed him as naïve, arguing that his background didn't prepare him for the rough-and-tumble of politics. But Zack had spent years navigating rejection in auditions, holding space for people's deepest wounds, and standing up for causes that weren't popular. He was no stranger to resistance. He met criticism head-on, not with arrogance, but with persistence. Each doubt thrown his way became a reason to dig deeper, to prove that authenticity could stand its ground against cynicism.

One defining moment came during his campaign for a seat on the London Assembly. Standing on a debate stage with representatives of established parties, Zack brought something different. He wasn't rehearsed to the point of sounding robotic, nor was he evasive when tough questions landed. Instead, he was direct, passionate, and grounded in real people's concerns. His words cut through the noise because they weren't crafted for headlines—they were drawn from experience. That authenticity set him apart, and voters noticed.

Winning a seat on the London Assembly was more than a personal victory; it was proof that his leap into politics had substance. It validated the belief that change was possible outside the traditional mold. For Zack, it wasn't about status—it was about responsibility. He carried into the Assembly the voices of the people he had met on doorsteps, the children wheezing in polluted neighborhoods, the tenants fighting unfair evictions, the workers worried about their future. Each decision, each question he raised, was rooted in those conversations.

Inside the Assembly, Zack's performance background revealed itself in new ways. Years of acting had trained him to command a room, to project his voice with confidence, and to engage audiences. But this time, the audience wasn't there for entertainment—it was there for accountability. He used his skills to demand answers, to challenge complacency, and to make sure critical issues like climate change and housing weren't brushed aside. The ability to hold attention wasn't about spotlight anymore; it was about pressure, applied on behalf of those who had none.

The leap into politics also brought personal transformation. Zack discovered that politics was not just about policy but about people—the alliances built, the trust earned, the communities empowered. He learned to navigate the balance between compromise and conviction, knowing when to hold firm and when to find common ground. He understood that resilience in politics wasn't about never bending, but about never breaking faith with those he represented.

Through it all, Zack never forgot why he leapt in the first place. It wasn't for titles or recognition. It was because he had seen too many lives held back by forces beyond individual control. He had listened to too many stories of injustice to stand by silently. The leap was an act of responsibility, a refusal to let fear of failure outweigh the possibility of impact.

Chapter Six

Finding a Home in the Green Party

political landscape, he saw something that didn't sit right with him. The big parties felt predictable, locked in old battles, too comfortable with half-measures and compromises that left ordinary people behind. Their platforms were polished, their campaigns well-funded, but their connection to people's lives felt shallow. For Zack, who had built his life around listening and responding to real human stories, that gap was impossible to ignore. If politics was meant to reflect the people it served, where was the honesty, the courage, the vision? That question pushed him toward the one party that seemed to match his restless conviction—the Greens.

The Green Party was not the most obvious choice. It wasn't the party of power brokers or career politicians. It lacked the machinery that guaranteed easy victories. What it did have, though, was authenticity. It had members who knocked on doors not for paychecks but because they believed the planet, and the people living on it, deserved better. It had activists who refused to treat climate change as an abstract issue and instead tied it directly to health, housing, jobs, and justice. That intersection—the place where environmental urgency met human dignity—was exactly where Zack felt at home.

Finding a home in the Green Party wasn't about convenience. It was about alignment. The Greens were talking about air pollution as a children's health crisis, not just an environmental statistic. They were calling out housing inequality as a form of systemic injustice, not just an economic inconvenience. They understood that politics wasn't about tinkering at the edges of broken systems but about asking bigger questions: What kind of society do we want to build? Who gets to feel safe, supported, and seen? Zack didn't just agree with those questions—he had been living them in his work as a therapist, activist, and performer.

When he joined, he wasn't greeted with the red carpets of establishment politics. What he found instead was community. Meetings held in community centers, back rooms of pubs, and shared spaces buzzed with energy. There was no pretense, no polished hierarchy. Ideas flowed freely, and members spoke with the urgency of people who knew time was short—short for the climate, short for families stuck in poverty, short for young people who couldn't wait decades for housing solutions. Zack thrived in that atmosphere. He didn't need to reinvent himself to fit in; he just needed to bring the skills and experiences he already carried.

That sense of belonging was matched by responsibility. The Greens demanded work. They expected their members to show up, to campaign, to engage with voters, to do the unglamorous labor of politics. For Zack, that wasn't a deterrent—it was a challenge. He canvassed neighborhoods, stood in the rain handing out leaflets, and joined rallies that received little media coverage but carried deep local significance. In those moments, he felt the essence of politics stripped down to its core: people talking to people, face to face, about the kind of world they wanted.

The Green Party also gave Zack a platform that felt honest. When he spoke under their banner, he didn't have to hide his convictions or soften his stance. He could connect environmental issues to social justice without being told it was "too radical." He could talk about inequality, housing, and mental health as interconnected crises without being pushed to stick to a narrow script. That freedom allowed him to bring his whole self into politics—his passion, his empathy, his insistence on authenticity.

But finding a home in the Green Party wasn't just about freedom; it was about impact. Zack quickly realized that while the Greens were small in numbers compared to the major parties, they carried a voice that was disproportionately powerful. In London, where issues of climate, housing, and transport converged, the Green

Party's message struck a nerve. People were ready to hear something different, something braver, something rooted in truth. Standing alongside fellow Greens, Zack felt part of a movement that was bigger than himself but also deeply personal.

The more he immersed himself, the more he saw how politics could be done differently. The Greens valued collaboration over competition. They encouraged open debate without tearing one another down. They treated leadership not as a prize but as a responsibility. For someone who had spent years in spaces where ego often dominated—whether on stage or in public debates—that culture of shared purpose was refreshing. It wasn't perfect, but it was real.

Zack's voice began to rise within the party, not because he chased the spotlight but because he resonated with people. He connected the dots between issues in a way that felt relatable. When he spoke about climate change, he didn't drown audiences in data. He told stories of children struggling with asthma near busy roads, of tenants shivering in poorly insulated homes, of workers commuting long hours because they couldn't afford to live near their jobs. He made the case that climate action wasn't just about saving the planet—it was about improving lives here and now.

This approach made him stand out. He wasn't trying to sound like a politician; he was trying to sound like a neighbor, a fellow citizen, someone who cared enough to step up. The Green Party valued that authenticity, and it propelled him into greater responsibility. His role grew from activist to candidate, from member to representative, but the roots remained the same: a belief in community, justice, and courage.

Inside the party, Zack also found himself inspired by those around him. The Green movement wasn't built by one person but by countless individuals willing to give their time, their energy, and their conviction. He saw young volunteers who poured themselves into campaigns after school or work. He met older members who had been fighting for environmental and social justice long before it became mainstream. Each encounter deepened his sense that he wasn't just part of a political party—he was part of a legacy, one that stretched back decades and pointed forward toward a more hopeful future.

As Zack grew into his role, the party grew with him. The Green Party was becoming more visible, more influential, more capable of challenging the dominance of old political forces. Being at the heart of that momentum was exhilarating. Zack wasn't content to stand still; he pushed for bold action, for a politics that refused to settle for "good enough." He understood that the Green Party's strength lay in its willingness to imagine differently and to demand more.

In finding a home in the Green Party, Zack Polanski found more than a political platform. He found a place where his values aligned with action, where his belief in people was matched by collective energy, where his sense of justice was not just respected but shared. For him, it wasn't just about joining a party—it was about joining a family of fighters, dreamers, and doers determined to prove that politics could be both principled and powerful.

Chapter Seven

A Voice for London

When Zack Polanski stepped into the chamber of the London Assembly, it wasn't just another career milestone. It was a responsibility he carried on behalf of millions who rarely felt heard. London, with all its energy, contradictions, and challenges, was more than just a city to him—it was a living, breathing story of people from every background imaginable. To be their representative meant more than debating policies; it meant becoming their voice in places where decisions too often felt distant and disconnected.

The Assembly itself was an intimidating stage. Long tables, formal procedures, and the weight of tradition could make it feel like a place designed to discourage ordinary voices. Yet Zack walked into that chamber with the same authenticity he had brought to community meetings and grassroots rallies. He wasn't there to blend in; he was there to ask sharper questions, push harder for answers, and insist that Londoners' concerns could not be swept aside by political pleasantries.

What set him apart from the beginning was his willingness to speak plainly. Too many politicians drowned their arguments in jargon, creating a wall between themselves and the public. Zack refused to play that game. When he asked the Mayor or other leaders about air quality, he didn't recite statistics in a vacuum—he talked about the child living on a busy street whose inhaler had become a permanent fixture in their backpack. When he pressed for housing reform, he described the tenant paying rent for a flat with mold crawling up the walls. He took issues often reduced to numbers and reattached them to human faces. That approach forced people in power to listen differently.

London had no shortage of problems demanding attention. Pollution choked busy roads. Housing costs pushed families out of neighborhoods they'd called home for generations. Public transportation remained a lifeline but often buckled under pressure. Mental health needs soared in a city moving at breakneck speed. Zack knew he couldn't solve all of it at once, but he also knew he couldn't ignore any of it. His role was to carry those issues into every discussion until they could no longer be brushed aside.

One of his earliest priorities was air quality. Londoners had been breathing dirty air for decades, but political responses had often been slow or half-hearted. Zack made it clear this wasn't a matter of abstract climate policy; it was about people's right to breathe. He demanded stronger measures, from cleaner transport to stricter regulations on polluters. When critics called the proposals too costly or disruptive, he reminded them of the hidden cost already being paid in hospital visits, lost workdays, and children growing up with damaged lungs. His insistence gave urgency to an issue many had treated as background noise.

Housing was another battlefield where Zack refused to stay quiet. In a city where wealth and poverty lived side by side, the gap had grown unbearable. Luxury apartments rose across the skyline, while countless residents struggled to find secure and affordable places to live. Zack spoke of renters trapped by exploitative landlords, of young professionals sharing cramped flats well into their thirties, of families forced out to the edges of the city, commuting hours each day just to make ends meet. He pressed for policies that prioritized people over profit—affordable housing, rent controls, and greater accountability for developers. For him, housing wasn't just an economic issue; it was about dignity, stability, and the basic right to call a place home.

But Zack's role wasn't only about raising problems. It was about proposing solutions that worked for real people. He supported sustainable transport options not because they sounded progressive, but because they made life easier—cheaper bus fares, safer cycling routes, and reliable trains that gave commuters back their time. He pushed for mental health resources in schools, arguing that prevention and support could save both lives and money. He linked environmental reforms to job creation, showing that a green economy wasn't a sacrifice but an opportunity. Every proposal came back to the same core principle: politics should serve people first.

Zack's ability to cut through political games became one of his strongest tools. Assembly sessions could sometimes descend into point-scoring, with parties more focused on outmaneuvering each other than on solving problems. Zack resisted that temptation. He asked direct questions, kept the spotlight on issues, and refused to let debates get lost in partisan noise. His style wasn't about winning arguments for the sake of headlines—it was about holding power accountable to the people outside the chamber.

The media began to notice his presence, not because he was flashy, but because he was consistent. He spoke with conviction but also with humanity. Interviews with him felt less like rehearsed statements and more like conversations with someone who cared deeply about the city. Journalists found in him a politician who could bridge the gap between the technical details of policy and the everyday realities of Londoners' lives. That visibility helped elevate both him and the Green Party, showing that even without the resources of larger parties, a strong voice could make an outsized impact.

Behind the scenes, Zack worked just as hard. He met with community groups, listened to activists, and sat with residents in boroughs across the city. He made it clear that his job wasn't to speak for Londoners from a distance, but to carry their words directly into City Hall. He treated every encounter as an opportunity to learn, to sharpen his understanding of what people were facing. That practice grounded him and ensured that his speeches in the chamber didn't drift into abstraction. They remained rooted in the voices of real Londoners.

There were moments of frustration, too. Change in politics was never fast enough. Proposals stalled, votes were lost, compromises diluted ambitious plans. Zack felt those setbacks deeply, but he also knew that persistence was part of the work. Each question asked, each demand repeated, each voice amplified contributed to a gradual shift. He believed that progress was built not on single victories but on relentless pressure, applied again and again until resistance gave way.

Over time, Zack's presence in the Assembly began to symbolize something larger. He wasn't just another elected official; he was proof that politics could sound different, act differently, and feel more connected. For Londoners tired of being treated as statistics or political pawns, his voice offered something rare: honesty paired with action.

And in a city as vast and complex as London, that honesty mattered. From the crowded buses in

Brixton to the leafy streets of Hampstead, from the markets of Camden to the high-rises of Canary Wharf, Londoners wanted to know that someone inside City Hall actually saw them. Zack Polanski became that someone.

Chapter Eight

The Rise of an Eco-Populist

The phrase eco-populist wasn't something Zack Polanski invented for himself. It emerged naturally, a description that stuck because it captured exactly what he represented. At a time when environmental politics often sounded technical, distant, or reserved for academics and policy wonks, Zack brought it down to street level. He talked about climate change not as a graph on a chart but as the smog in a child's lungs, the rising rent in drafty apartments, the jobs disappearing as industries clung to outdated systems. He gave the green agenda a human pulse.

For years, environmentalists had battled a stereotype: well-meaning but out of touch, more interested in saving polar bears than fixing broken boilers in working-class homes. Zack shattered that caricature. He showed that green politics could be gritty, urgent, and rooted in the struggles of ordinary people. His message was simple: the fight for the planet and the fight for justice were the same fight. Clean air, fair housing, reliable transit, affordable energy—all were issues that affected daily life, and all were connected to how society treated the environment. That framing gave environmental politics a fresh energy, and Zack became its voice.

On the campaign trail, this style was evident in every conversation. He didn't approach voters with leaflets full of abstract promises. Instead, he asked questions. How was their rent? How was their commute? Were they worried about their kids' health? People were often surprised when Zack linked those answers back to climate and environmental reform. He had a way of weaving their personal experiences into a larger story about a city and a planet in transition. By the time he finished, the dots were connected—what had felt like separate frustrations now appeared as part of one bigger picture.

Critics sometimes tried to paint him as idealistic, but Zack's approach was anything but detached from reality. He used the language of everyday life, avoiding the elitism that often kept environmentalism in a bubble. When he talked about solar power, he talked about lowering utility bills. When he advocated for public transit, he pointed to how much money people would save compared to owning a car. When he demanded insulation for housing, he emphasized warmer homes, lower costs, and fewer illnesses in winter. This populist framing made the environmental agenda accessible and urgent. It wasn't about abstract ideals—it was about better lives here and now.

Inside the London Assembly, his eco-populist voice became sharper. He pressed for ambitious policies, but he never lost sight of how they landed on people's doorsteps. Debates about carbon reduction targets weren't just statistics to him; they were opportunities to argue for cleaner buses in South London or safer walking routes for schoolchildren. Even when the topics grew technical, Zack grounded them in stories that humanized the issue. That ability to connect macro-scale problems with micro-scale realities gave his arguments weight. It made it harder for opponents to dismiss him as just another idealist.

The term "eco-populist" also reflected his style of politics beyond policy. He made himself accessible, attending community events in boroughs far from the spotlight of central London. He stood on street corners with campaigners handing out flyers, long after other politicians had left for photo ops. He showed up to protests, not as a guest speaker above the crowd, but as another body in the march. His willingness to stand shoulder to shoulder with activists reinforced the populist side of his politics—he wasn't positioning himself above the people; he was positioning himself with them.

This authenticity made him both a target and a force to be reckoned with. Opponents tried to frame him as radical, warning that his ideas would disrupt business and scare off investors. Zack countered by pointing out that the status quo was already costly—that air pollution was killing Londoners, that housing inequality was destabilizing communities, that reliance on fossil fuels was an economic gamble. His eco-populism turned the tables, asking why people should continue paying the price for political cowardice.

Media outlets began to highlight this contrast. Where some politicians stumbled over climate policy talking points, Zack delivered sound bites that were relatable, sharp, and memorable. He didn't come across as rehearsed, yet his words carried weight. "Why should a child in Tower Hamlets grow up with a shorter life expectancy because politicians refuse to act?" That kind of framing hit harder than numbers ever could. It cut straight to values, and values were what eco-populism was all about.

As Zack's profile grew, so did the expectations. Voters, activists, and colleagues looked to him for leadership, not just advocacy. That shift demanded balance. He had to hold on to the firebrand energy that drew people in while also navigating the practical demands of policymaking. Eco-populism, in his hands, wasn't about empty promises or slogans. It was about pressing relentlessly until the gap between ideals and action narrowed. That persistence was what made him stand out—not just his ability to inspire, but his refusal to let inspiration fade once the cameras were gone.

The strength of his eco-populist approach was most visible during moments of resistance. When proposals for stricter environmental measures were attacked as unaffordable or unrealistic, Zack flipped the narrative. What was unaffordable, he asked, about children missing school because of asthma? What was unrealistic about expecting homes that didn't make tenants sick? He reframed costs as investments, reframed ambition as responsibility. In doing so, he made eco-politics not just a vision for the future but a demand for justice in the present.

The rise of Zack Polanski as an eco-populist also highlighted a generational shift. Younger Londoners, facing precarious work, impossible housing markets, and a climate crisis bearing down on their future, found in him a politician who didn't sugarcoat their reality but also didn't surrender to despair. His message carried urgency but also possibility. It said: yes, the challenges are massive, but yes, we still have agency if we choose courage over complacency. That duality—fearless about the scale of the problem, but optimistic about human potential—was the heart of his eco-populism.

At its core, Zack's rise was about trust. People believed him not because he had the loudest voice but because he spoke in a way that reflected their lives. He didn't pretend that politics had easy answers, but he made clear that answers had to come from standing with people, not above them. That is what it meant to be an eco-populist: to turn environmental politics into a common cause, a shared struggle, a movement that belonged to everyone.

Chapter Nine

Leadership, Vision, and the Fight for Justice

Leadership is often misunderstood as the ability to command a room or to speak louder than everyone else. For Zack Polanski, leadership meant something different. It meant standing alongside others, amplifying voices that had been ignored, and never forgetting that the purpose of power was to serve. When he rose to the role of Deputy Leader of the Green Party, he carried with him not the arrogance of ambition, but the humility of someone who knew leadership was a responsibility, not a crown.

His vision for leadership came from lived experience. He had been the outsider, the man who didn't come from a family of politicians or a polished pipeline of privilege. He had been the actor navigating rejection, the therapist listening to raw pain, the activist holding a megaphone on rain-soaked streets. Those experiences shaped his understanding that leadership wasn't about appearing untouchable. It was about being relatable, resilient, and accountable.

As Deputy Leader, Zack used his platform to sharpen the Green Party's message, but he did it with a style that made politics feel less like a lecture and more like a dialogue. He avoided talking down to people. He listened first, spoke second, and never treated criticism as an attack to dodge but as an opportunity to engage. This approach made him stand out in a political world dominated by rehearsed lines and rigid sound bites.

His vision was bold, but it was also practical. He believed the fight for justice wasn't separate from the fight for climate—it was the same battle fought on different fronts. He tied environmental policy directly to economic fairness, housing security, healthcare access, and human dignity. To Zack, the Green Party's work wasn't about pushing an "alternative" agenda. It was about placing justice at the center of political life.

In speeches across the country, Zack returned again and again to the theme of justice. Justice for communities breathing toxic air. Justice for renters trapped by exploitative landlords. Justice for young people denied opportunities because of broken systems. His leadership pushed the Green Party to frame its mission not only as a fight for the planet but as a fight for people who had been silenced by years of inequality. He believed that environmental justice without social justice was incomplete, and he worked tirelessly to merge the two into a vision that resonated with wider audiences.

This vision meant embracing challenges head-on. In debates, Zack refused to let opponents dismiss the Greens as unrealistic. When critics claimed environmental policies would harm the economy, he countered with facts about green jobs, renewable energy industries, and long-term savings for households. When detractors argued that justice issues were beyond the Greens' reach, he reminded them that political change always starts small, with voices willing to demand more than the mainstream believes possible. His fight was never about being the loudest; it was about being the most consistent, the most authentic, and the most unwilling to give up.

But leadership also meant inspiring those around him. Zack didn't position himself as the sole driver of the party's progress. He uplifted grassroots campaigners, volunteers, and local candidates, making sure their stories and their work were visible. He knew the Green Party's strength came from its members—the people who knocked on doors after work, who handed out leaflets on weekends, who stood in council chambers demanding cleaner air and safer housing. His role, as he saw it, was to connect their energy to a bigger vision.

The fight for justice demanded courage, and Zack didn't shy away from confrontation. He challenged developers who treated housing as a commodity instead of a necessity. He pressed leaders on their failures to address London's polluted air. He spoke out on mental health, calling for a system that treated it with the same seriousness as physical health. In each fight, he wasn't afraid to name the forces standing in the way of progress. That candor drew criticism from some, admiration from others, but always attention.

What made Zack's leadership resonate was his refusal to separate politics from humanity. He didn't speak of policies as abstract concepts; he grounded them in personal stories. When talking about climate, he mentioned the child with asthma living by a congested road. When arguing for housing reform, he told of renters paying outrageous sums for unsafe flats. When calling for fairer wages, he pointed to families juggling multiple jobs yet still unable to get by. His vision for justice wasn't theoretical—it was lived.

The fight wasn't easy. Political victories were often incremental, and setbacks came frequently. But Zack's resilience never wavered. He had built a life around reinvention, and in politics, that adaptability became an asset. When doors closed, he knocked again. When proposals failed, he reintroduced them with sharper arguments. When he faced personal attacks, he leaned on authenticity and honesty to weather them. Leadership, to Zack, wasn't about avoiding failure—it was about refusing to be defined by it.

In his role, he also redefined what it meant to be a political leader in the modern age. While others carefully curated personas, Zack leaned into transparency. He shared not only successes but frustrations, not only polished lines but genuine reflections. This openness allowed people to see him not as a distant figure but as someone willing to admit imperfection while still pushing forward. That vulnerability, rare in politics, made him more relatable and strengthened his credibility.

The fight for justice under Zack's leadership extended beyond London. He traveled across the country, lending his voice to local campaigns and showing solidarity with communities often overlooked by national leaders. Whether in small towns battling environmental destruction or in cities demanding fairer housing, he carried the same message: justice was not negotiable, and the Green Party was here to fight for it.

His leadership style reflected a belief in collective progress. He wasn't trying to be the star of the movement. Instead, he wanted to be the thread that tied people together, the spark that turned individual frustrations into shared action. That was the essence of his vision: leadership that empowered, politics that listened, justice that included everyone.

Chapter Ten

Hope as a Political Force

Hope is often dismissed in politics as something soft, sentimental, or naïve. For Zack Polanski, it was none of those things. He understood hope as a form of energy, a weapon as sharp as any policy paper, and a driving force that could move people from frustration to action. Where others saw hope as a dream, Zack saw it as a strategy—one that could rebuild trust in politics and give ordinary people the courage to demand better.

He didn't stumble into this belief by accident. Growing up, he had experienced first-hand what it felt like when institutions seemed distant and politics appeared irrelevant. He had also felt the crushing weight of rejection during his acting career, and the heavy silence of despair that echoed through his therapy sessions with clients. Again and again, he saw how hopelessness shrank people, kept them small, and convinced them that nothing could change. But just as often, he saw what happened when people were offered hope—not empty optimism, but a vision tied to action. They stood taller, they spoke louder, and they began to see themselves as part of something larger.

This realization shaped his political style. While many politicians thrived on fear—fear of outsiders, fear of loss, fear of failure—Zack leaned into possibility. His speeches often carried a rhythm of what could be: cleaner air in the lungs of every child, affordable housing that didn't drain paychecks, a climate policy that preserved futures instead of erasing them. He didn't shy away from naming problems, but he refused to let the problems have the final word. Hope was always the pivot.

To Zack, hope wasn't passive. It was radical. It challenged the status quo by insisting that a better world was not only imaginable but achievable. When he stood in community halls or at rallies, he didn't ask people to simply trust him—he asked them to trust themselves, to believe that their voices could rewrite the rules. That was the force of his message: hope wasn't about waiting for someone else to deliver change. It was about claiming the power to build it together.

This approach resonated because it was honest. Hope, in Zack's hands, never felt like sugar-coating reality. He didn't deny that the challenges were immense—climate collapse, inequality, broken housing systems, disillusionment with government. Instead, he spoke plainly about how hard the work would be, while simultaneously offering a vision of why the work mattered. That balance made his words credible. People could sense that he wasn't trying to sell them a fantasy. He was inviting them into a fight that was both urgent and winnable.

Hope also defined how Zack approached leadership within the Green Party. In internal meetings, he often reminded colleagues that despair was the greatest gift they could give their opponents. If people believed nothing would change, then the powerful had already won. But if people believed even a little that change was possible, doors opened. Campaigners worked longer, volunteers showed up on rainy Saturdays, and voters took the leap of supporting a party that didn't always have the resources of its rivals. For Zack, nurturing that spark of hope was just as essential as drafting manifestos.

One of his most memorable moments came during a campaign event where he spoke about children growing up in London's most polluted neighborhoods. Instead of leading with statistics, he described a little boy he had met whose inhaler was never far from reach. The boy's mother worried every night about whether his lungs would hold out in adulthood. After painting this picture, Zack looked at the audience and said, "It doesn't have to be this way. Imagine a London where every child breathes clean air. That's not fantasy—that's policy, if we decide to make it so." The room went quiet, then erupted in applause. People weren't just moved—they were mobilized. That was hope, wielded like a political tool.

What separated Zack's vision from hollow inspiration was his insistence on action. He didn't ask people to hope in the abstract; he tied it to concrete steps. Join a campaign. Write to your representative. Support local candidates. Show up at council meetings. For him, hope was fuel, but action was the engine. Without action, hope was just a flicker. With action, it became fire.

This belief in hope as a political force also set him apart in a cynical age. Politics had become, for many, a theater of broken promises and endless scandals. Voters were weary of slogans that led nowhere and leaders who spoke of change but delivered very little. Zack's willingness to center hope didn't ignore this cynicism—it confronted it. By acknowledging why people felt disillusioned, he made space for them to imagine something better.

And by embodying that possibility in his own journey—an actor turned therapist turned politician—he showed that reinvention was possible not only for individuals but for entire systems.

Even his critics, those who dismissed him as idealistic, often underestimated the power of his approach. They mistook hope for weakness. But Zack understood that hope demanded more strength than despair. It required perseverance when things got hard, resilience when setbacks piled up, and creativity when old strategies failed. To stand before a crowd battered by years of disappointment and still speak of what was possible—that was courage.

For Zack, hope was also about connection. He often spoke about how politics should not just be about policies written in offices but about lives lived in communities. Hope meant listening as much as speaking, and building trust across divides. It meant finding common ground in unexpected places—between environmentalists and trade unionists, between housing campaigners and climate activists, between young people demanding a future and older generations holding memories of past struggles. Hope was the thread that tied these groups together, weaving their stories into a broader movement.

He believed hope could cut through polarization. In a world where anger and division dominated headlines, he offered an alternative. Not bland consensus, but a sense that differences didn't have to end in hostility. Hope was the reminder that people wanted many of the same things: dignity, security, clean air, fair wages, a livable future. By grounding politics in those shared desires, Zack offered a vision that could unite rather than divide.

This philosophy carried him beyond formal politics. When speaking to students, he encouraged them to see themselves as leaders, no matter their age or background. When meeting with activists, he reminded them that their efforts were part of a longer story of struggle and progress. When addressing disillusioned citizens, he urged them not to give up on democracy but to reclaim it. Each of these conversations planted seeds of hope, seeds that he believed would grow long after speeches ended or campaigns concluded.

Zack Polanski's political journey showed that hope, when taken seriously, could be as practical as it was powerful. It wasn't a slogan for him—it was a discipline. A refusal to surrender to despair. A determination to see possibilities where others only saw obstacles. And above all, a belief that hope, in the hands of ordinary people, could move mountains.

Conclusion

Dear Reader,

You've just taken a journey through the life of Zack Polanski—a journey of resilience, reinvention, courage, and unshakable hope. And as we reach this final page, it's important to say this: you are the true force that gives meaning to every word written here.

A biography is more than the story of one individual. It is a bridge between a life lived and the hearts and minds of those willing to listen. Without your time, your curiosity, and your willingness to dive into these pages, this book would be nothing more than paper and ink. It's your engagement that brings these chapters alive. It's your imagination that walks beside Zack through the streets of Salford, sits with him in the theater, and marches with him into the halls of politics.

You invested your energy, your resources, and your most precious commodity—your time—into understanding this story. That is no small thing. In a world overflowing with noise, distraction, and endless choices, you chose to be here, reading, reflecting, and allowing this journey to matter. For that, I want to thank you not just politely, but profoundly. You are the heartbeat of this book.

Zack's life is one of determination and vision, but it is also a reminder that stories don't exist in isolation. They exist because people like you choose to read them, share them, and carry them forward. Every sentence you've read is only complete when it meets your interpretation. Every moment of Zack's path gains new meaning because you cared enough to walk it alongside him. That is the quiet but extraordinary power you hold as a reader.

And now, as we close this book together, I want to humbly ask for your support. If this story moved you, inspired you, or even challenged the way you see politics, resilience, or hope, please take a moment to leave a positive review. Your words matter more than you might realize. They help other readers discover this journey, they encourage writers to keep creating, and they ensure that stories like Zack Polanski's reach the people who need them most.

Think of your review not as a formality, but as a gift—a way to extend the life of this book beyond your own reading. It is your chance to say, this mattered to me, and it might matter to you too. That single act of generosity can make all the difference.

So, from the very first chapter to this last word, thank you. Thank you for trusting this book with your time. Thank you for choosing to engage with Zack's story. And thank you, in advance, for leaving a review that will help this biography live on in the hands of many more readers to come.

Because without you, dear reader, this book is incomplete. With you, it becomes unforgettable.

Printed in Dunstable, United Kingdom